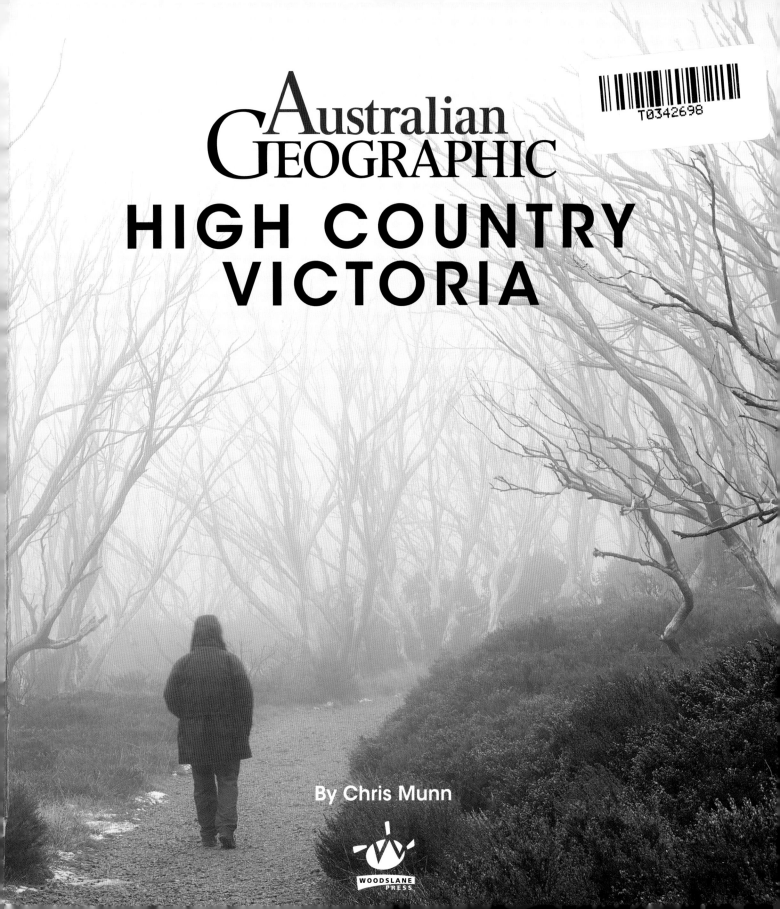

Australian Geographic
HIGH COUNTRY VICTORIA

By Chris Munn

WOODSLANE PRESS

Woodslane Press Pty Ltd
10 Apollo Street
Warriewood, NSW 2102
Email: info@woodslane.com.au
Tel: 02 8445 2300 Website: www.woodslane.com.au

First published in Australia in 2020 by Woodslane Press in association with Australian Geographic
© 2020 Woodslane Press, photographs © Australian Geographic and others
(see acknowledgements on page 62)

NATIONAL LIBRARY OF AUSTRALIA

A catalogue record for this book is available from the National Library of Australia

Printed in China by Asia Pacific Offset
Front Cover Image : Chris Munn (Craig's Hut)
Rear Cover Image : Craig Lewis (Snow Daisies)
Book design by: Christine Schiedel

CONTENTS

THE HIGH COUNTRY

The Victorian High Country is an enchanting region which encompasses Mount Baw Baw in the south, Falls Creek and Mount Hotham in the north, while reaching out across the rolling hills and picturesque valleys below to Rutherglen in the west and Corryong on its eastern outer fringe. At its heart lies Victoria's majestic alps, home to the state's alpine resorts, a dramatic landscape graced by spring wildflowers and blanketed by snow in winter. Pristine streams meander, at times plunging dramatically over escarpments into deep gorges, while weathered cattlemen's huts can be found sheltering amongst stands of gnarled snow gums on windswept alpine meadows.

Amongst the foothills rest idyllic towns like Beechworth and Yackandandah, born out of the Victorian gold rush of the 1850s, both radiating a charm of yesteryear. A land steeped in legend the past is ever present, with shadows of ancient indigenous people, gold miners and notorious bushrangers like Ned Kelly continuing to linger across their old haunts.

Bushwalking is an ever-popular way to experience the High Country's hidden gems and reconnect with nature. Trail running, rail trails, mountain biking, hang gliding and hot air ballooning await the adventurous. Lovers of history will lose themselves amongst historic buildings and local museums where events and faces of the past are lovingly given life. Farmers markets and festivals celebrate the changing of seasons and local produce while the cellar doors of local wineries beckon the visiting wine connoisseur.

The High Country is a landscape of many moods, with snow and freezing conditions possible at any time of year. Always be prepared with warm, waterproof clothing. Let somebody know where you are going and when you will return.

Above: As you begin exploring the High Country, you will quickly discover one of its great charms: old cottages and sheds, slowly surrendering to the ravages of time, standing amidst idyllic settings.

Left: The Victorian High Country is home to an abundance of wildlife including alpine dingos, mountain pygmy-possums and wild mountain brumbies. At dawn and dusk, sightings of eastern grey kangaroos and wombats are very likely.

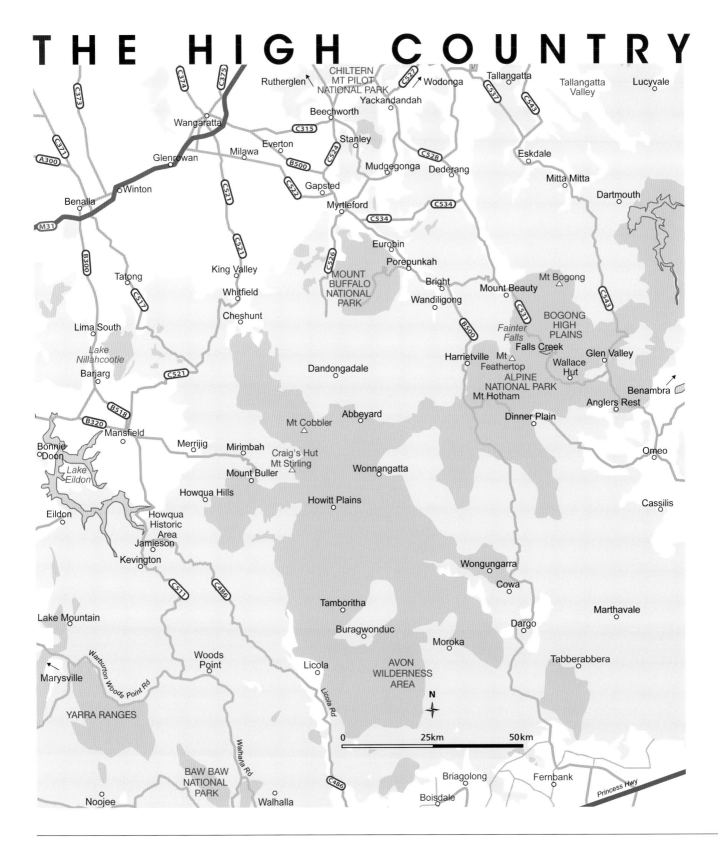

Right: The walking track to Fainter Falls (1.5km, 40 minutes return) begins opposite the car park, just before the Bogong High Plains Road crosses Fainter Creek on the way to Falls Creek. The track is formed, but there are some hills to contend with.

Below: The High Country is home to one of Victoria's magnificent touring routes, the Great Alpine Road. Starting at Wangaratta, it passes through picturesque towns such as Myrtleford, Bright and Harrietville before climbing over Mount Hotham, through Omeo and onto Bairnsdale.

GEOLOGY

The story of the Victorian High Country begins long ago during the Jurassic Period, at a time when the Australian landmass still lay within the ancient super continent of Gondwana. Dinosaurs roamed the earth and despite being located near the South Pole, Australia was relatively warm, with temperate forests covering the landscape. As forces deep within the planet began to drive its tectonic plates apart, continental drift saw Gondwana separate, with Australia, Antarctica and New Zealand the final remnant of the ancient continent. Drifting northwards from Antarctica during the late Cretaceous Period, Australia and New Zealand too parted ways.

With the stretching and thinning of the crust, magma deep within the earth's mantle pushed upwards creating a large plateau, then as New Zealand pulled further away, the plateau collapsed creating a great rift valley which was later inundated by the Tasman sea, forming the east coast of Southern Australia. In time, rain, wind, snow and ice would erode the high plateau, dissecting the landscape by carving out river plains and deep valleys, leaving the peaks and high plains we know today. Volcanic activity was prevalent across the High Country, with striking columnar basalt to be found on the Bogong High Plains and at Falls Creek. The Mt Buffalo and Baw Baw plateaus are unique amongst the Alps, the only examples of late Devonian magma chambers which failed to breach the earth's surface, cooling deep underground and later exposed by erosion.

Above: Amidst the rolling Bogong High Plains you will discover fascinating columnar basalt formations, a legacy of ancient volcanic activity which helped form the Victorian Alps.

Left: As softer sedimentary rock has eroded, exposing the granite below, beautiful gorges and waterfalls have been carved into the landscape around Beechworth. The stained granite of Woolshed Falls is particularly vibrant in colour after rainfall.

CLIMATE

The High Country may be a long way from the coast, yet, like most of Victoria, the region's climate is shaped by weather patterns originating from the Southern Ocean. Summer high pressure systems push lows south towards Antarctica, bringing warm sunny days with average temperatures of 28°C to towns like Bright and Mansfield, while the high plains enjoy a milder 16°C. With winter approaching, highs track further to the north as the first strong cold fronts pass through the region bringing subzero temperatures to the Alps and milder maximums of 8°C to the valleys. Being a landscape of diverse geography, the conditions across the High Country can vary dramatically at any given time. Long days, warm temperatures and sunshine make summer a perfect time to discover the charm of historic towns like Wandiligong or for fishing on Lake Eildon. Autumn is a time of deciduous colour, mild days and cool nights as the first hint of woodsmoke from open fires lingers in the afternoon air. Cold and moody, winter sees rainfall increasing as blizzards bring snow to the Alps, with August often the best month for snow sports. A time of dynamic weather and renewal, spring sees wildflowers bloom across the High Country while melting snow feeds waterfalls which are just waiting to be explored.

SUMMER
■ (December - February)
The days are long and sunshine is plentiful with daytime temperatures nearing 30°C in the valleys and 16°C high in the Alps. Summer storms can be intense and short term heatwaves can exceed 40°C. This is a great time of year to rise early and explore the region's rail trails.

AUTUMN
■ (March - May)
Mild days and cool nights with maximum temperatures between 10°C in the Alps and 20°C in the valleys below make autumn a wonderful time of year. Explore the autumn colour of towns like Bright or tour the region's famous wineries.

WINTER
■ (June – August),
Winter is the coldest and wettest season, with the area around Mt Baw Baw recording an average of up to 500mm of rainfall. Maximum temperatures in the valleys average 12°C while the snow-covered Alps can drop well below freezing. Rug up and embrace the fresh, crisp winter air with a trip to one of the alpine resorts for a little snow play.

SPRING
■ (September to November)
Spring is a time of transition and contradictions with early periods of warm, dry weather broken by intense cold fronts bring a final burst of wintery weather. Average daily temperatures across the region range from 9-20°C making spring a great time to explore farmers markets and sample local produce.

Right: As the days grow shorter and temperatures begin to fall, overnight cold snaps see autumn colour emerge across the Buckland Valley.

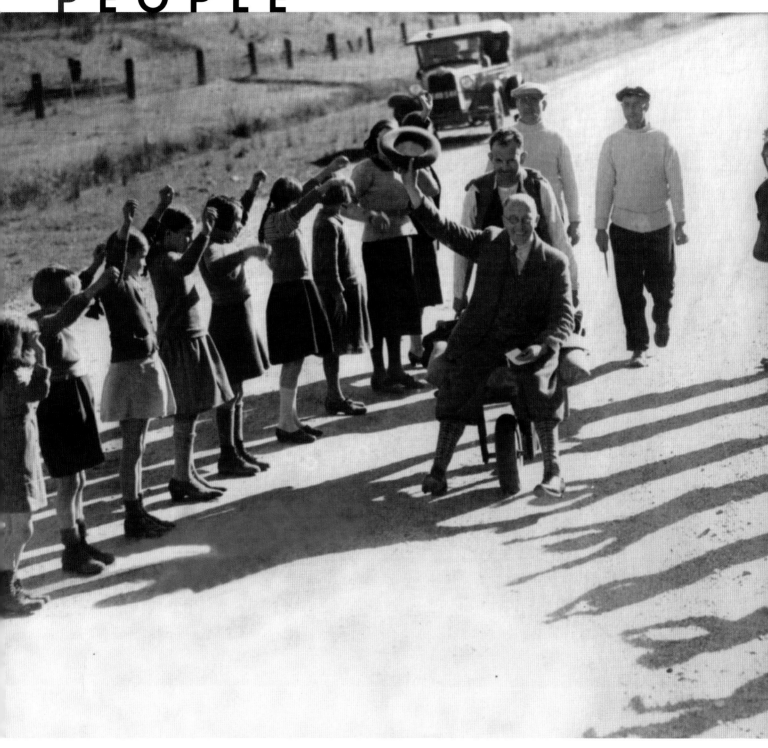

Left: Children from Eurobin State School cheer Tom Parkinson and Sydney Evens on their quest to Mount Buffalo. The famous wheelbarrow can be seen at Beechworth's Burke Museum.

Below: A large number of Chinese miners made their way to the goldfields of the Victorian High Country in the 1850s. Sadly for some, they never returned home. Beechworth Cemetery honours their memory with a large Chinese section and beautifully preserved burning towers.

For well over 10,000 years the ancient ancestors of tribes including the Minjambuta, Duduroa, Jaitmathang and Taungurung thrived, living at one with the land and moving with the seasons. The first Europeans to visit the High Country were explorers Hume and Hovell in 1824 who, while passing to the east of present day Wangaratta named "Mount Buffalo" believing it to resemble a sleeping buffalo. Pastoralists moved into the area in the 1830s and 40s, introducing cattle and sheep. With lush grasses waiting on the high plains, pastoralists began a tradition of summer alpine grazing from the 1830s onward, building a network of cattle yards and rustic bush huts. With gold discovered in the Ovens Valley, Buckland Valley and Omeo in the 1850s towns like Bright and Beechworth quickly grew, with thousands heading to the diggings. The mid 1800s also saw the emergence of the bushranger, with larger than life Harry Power claiming to have performed more than 600 robberies in 1869. Railways, the timber industry and later tourism would all impact population shape and growth in the High Country. The region has been home to many remarkable characters, but few are remembered like Tom Parkinson and Sydney Evans. Both from Beechworth, Parkinson wagered that he could push Evans in a wheelbarrow from Beechworth to the chalet on Mount Buffalo within 8 days. Affectionately remembered as the 'Wheelbarrow Derby', the event saw Beechworth observe a public holiday in celebration as they set off in 1935. Finishing in the snow, Parkinson won the wager, and to this day the winner's cheque has never been cashed.

ECONOMY

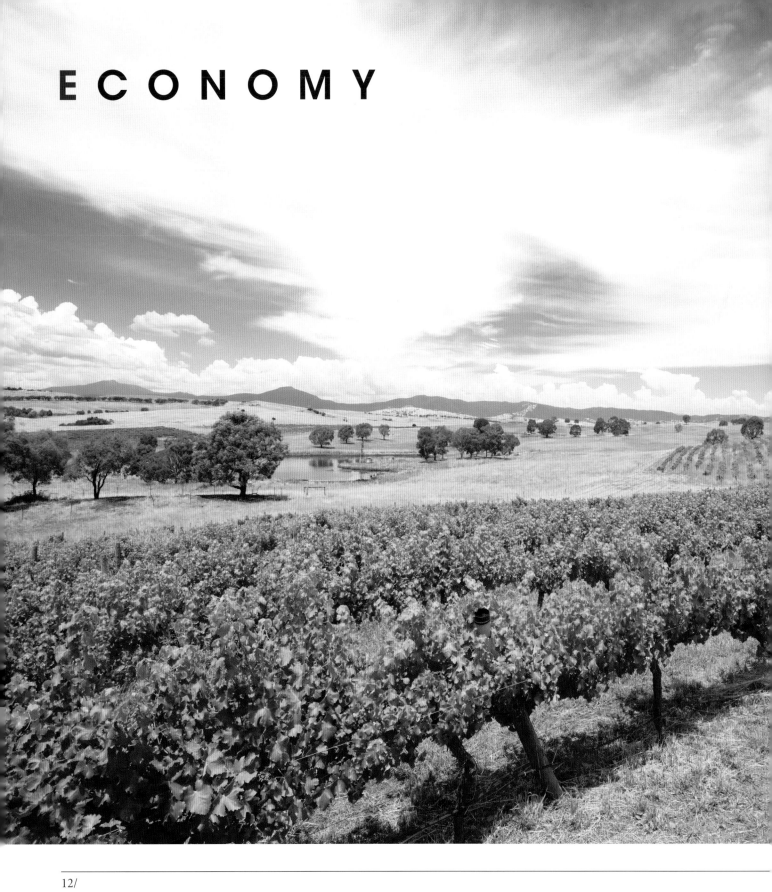

Exploring the Victorian High Country, you quickly realise that it covers a vast geographic region, which falls within the boundaries of many local government areas including the Mansfield, Alpine, Indigo, Towong and East Gippsland shires. Opened up by pastoralists in the early 1830s it is little surprise that agriculture, forestry and fishing have become major industries for the region. Between dairy cows grazing in the Kiewa Valley, pine plantations growing around Bright and vineyards on the outskirts of Mansfield, agriculture adds $1 billion dollars to the local economy. In addition to agriculture, construction is growing in importance for Mansfield as demand for new housing drives the sector. For shires such as Indigo, manufacturing is also becoming important, employing up to 25% of its workforce.

With a unique value proposition of history, festivals, markets, natural beauty and alpine ski resorts, the Victorian High Country has long been a popular tourist destination. Although not an industry in its own right, the so called 'visitor economy' is an important contributor to the retail, food and accommodation sectors. In the 2016-17 ski season alone, Victoria's alpine resorts drew over 700,000 visitors to the region, sustaining employment for 4,500 people and injecting $500 million into the local economy. Visitor numbers can only grow and as they increase so too will the benefits to local businesses.

Above: Winter is a significant event in the Victorian High Country, drawing large crowds and powering the visitor economy both up the mountains and in the surrounding towns.

Left: Agriculture is a significant contributor to the economy of the Victorian High Country. With perfect conditions, the region is home to a large number of wineries.

CULTURE

For well over 10,000 years people such as the Minjambuta, Dudu-roa, Jaitmathang and Taungu-rung lived in harmony with the Victorian High Country. With an intimate knowledge of geography, plant and animal life they moved with the seasons through the valleys, river flats, high plains and foothills as their food sources flourished. Summer in particular was an important season, as bogong moths, originating on the plains of Southern Queensland, migrated to the Victorian Alps, hibernating amongst crevices and rocky outcrops. Gathering at the foothills, local groups and those from afar would ascend the Bogong High Plains, Mount Buffalo and Mount Buller to feast on the moths and conduct ceremonies such as marriages, trading and resolving disputes. It was also a deeply spiritual time when elders would take younger men to the peaks and share stories of the dreamtime. Unfortunately, with pastoralists moving into the region by the 1830s, fences were erected where indigenous people once travelled freely and, inevitably, conflicts arose. Gold mining also had a disastrous impact on the waterways and native forests, decimating food sources. In a few short years indigenous populations would be devastated due to displacement and disease. While the ancient clans may no longer cross the valleys or high plains, their story lives on amidst rock art like the thylacine painted in red ochre at Mount Pilot, artefacts scattered throughout the Alps and the names of majestic mountain peaks such as the 'Big Fella', Mount Bogong.

■ Left: The Mansfield scarred tree is an important relic of the Taungurung people who lived amongst the valleys and hills of the region for thousands of years. Cutting away bark from the trunk of this tree for a canoe, they have left behind the scar we see today.

The alpine dingo slinking across Mount Buffalo's snow-covered plateau and the platypus foraging for food in the Delatite River may be worlds apart, yet both have found their niche within the extremes of the Victorian High Country. For some species, however, there is a fine line between survival and extinction, with the Baw Baw frog, Leadbeater's possum and the mountain pygmy-possum all critically endangered. Thought to be extinct until rediscovered in 1966, the mountain pygmy possum is the only marsupial to live solely within the sub-alpine and alpine zones with known populations between Mount Bogong and Mount Hotham as well as at Mount Buller. Hibernating during the coldest periods of winter, they live in rocky areas with the females at higher altitude where food is more plentiful. In summer the sight of bogong moths swarming is spectacular, arriving each year from the north they hibernate amongst the cool granite caves and crevices of the Alps. Dusk is always a great time to spot wildlife such as kangaroos, wallabies and wombats as they seek out water and feed amongst the lowlands and foothills of the Alps. Birdlife abounds across the High Country with gang-gang cockatoos, crimson rosellas, flame robins, yellow-faced honeyeaters, kookaburras and majestic wedge tail eagles to be seen. On warmer days keep an eye out for snakes, with tiger, brown, white-lipped and highlands copper heads common. Of all the animals to be found in the High Country, it is ironically the non-native brumbies roaming the high plains which most resonate with the national identity. The sight of a mob galloping in the distance on the Bogong High Plains powerfully evokes the legends of the High Country cattlemen.

Opposite page: With a call some liken to the sound of a rusty gate, the gang-gang cockatoo can grow to 37cm in length. Females are distinguished by a chest of red feathers, while males have a brilliant red plumage covering their head. Preferring the tall trees of montane forests, they can also be found in snow gum woodlands. Creatures of habit, gang-gangs will often return to nest in the same tree.

Below: Each year billions of bogong moths take flight, escaping the summer heat to shelter in granite caves and crevices of the Alps. Nutty in flavour, the moths are a major food source for the mountain pygmy-possum and not so long ago provided important nutrients to indigenous people who ascended the Alps each year to feast on them.

WILDLIFE

Left: At sunrise and sunset their distinctive call can he heard across the High Country, seemingly laughing at the world around them. The largest member of the kingfisher family, the laughing kookaburra lives in open woodlands on a diet including insects, snakes and lizards.

Right: Adorable and universally loved, koalas sped up to 20 hours a day sleeping and most of their waking hours eating. Keep an eye out as you explore the High Country, at times they can appear in unexpected locations such as the streets of Beechworth.

Below right: Brumbies have been running wild across the Victorian High Country for well over a century. Thousands of hoof prints can be found on the land behind Hotham Airport, while descendants of mobs bred by Osborn Young in the late 1800s still roam Pretty Valley on the Bogong High Plains.

Below left: Growing up to 2 metres, eastern brown snakes are highly venomous and come in a wide range of colours. The young are distinctive, with black heads and dark vertical stripes along the length of the body.

PLANTLIFE

Across the lowlands of the Victorian High Country, 19th century pastoralists and gold miners have had a significant impact on the region's plant life, clearing much of the native forests with only remnant tracts to be found today. As populations grew and towns developed, ornamental deciduous trees such as poplars, maples, elms and liquidambers were planted extensively and as a result Bright, Beechworth, Mansfield and Mount Beauty are spectacular during autumn.

Amongst the mountains, as elevation increases, temperatures drop and snowfalls prevail, there are noticeable transitions in vegetation. Tall montane forests dominate the lower slopes with mountain ash predominant, its understory of ferns and wattle seen across the Alps. Myrtle beech nestled amongst cool temperate rainforest is present amongst valleys on the Baw Baw Plateau. Above 1500 metres closed heathlands and snow gum woodlands dominate the subalpine zone. A remarkable tree, the snow gum develops a unique gnarled appearance as it grows away from the wind with many fascinating examples on the Bogong High Plains and slopes of Mount Stirling. Within the alpine zone above 1800 metres, the climate is at its most extreme: trees do not generally grow and low-lying open heathland and herbfields flourish. Naturally spring and summer is a time for wildflowers, with billy buttons, snow daisies and a wide array of other species blooming across the Victorian Alps.

Far left: Liquidambers are a common sight across the lowlands of the Victorian High Country. A spectacular deciduous tree native to North America, its star shaped leaves shift from lush greens to rich hues of red, gold and deep burgundy in autumn.

Left: After the monochrome tones of winter, wildflowers carpet the Victorian Alps during spring and summer, with the bright yellow flower of the alpine everlasting adding a magnificent touch of colour to the landscape.

Below Left: Capable of growing in seemingly impossible locations, snow gums are the ultimate survivor of the Victorian Alps. In autumn they shed their bark, wet weather drawing out otherwise muted shades of yellow and red, while heavy snowfall sees their limbs bow under the weight rather than breaking.

YACKANDANDAH

Affectionately known to locals as Yack, Yackandandah lies 30 kilometres to the south of Wodonga on the edge of Stanley State Forest, looking out across the picturesque Ben Valley. The childhood home of the first Australian born governor-general Sir Isaac Isaacs, Yackandandah owes its origins to the discovery of gold at the junction of Yackandandah and Commissioners Creeks in 1852. With news of fresh gold finds difficult to hide, word spread quickly and a small settlement of tents and timber buildings soon developed. Surveyed in 1856, Yackandandah's High Street began to take shape with new structures joining those of James Cardwell's Star Hotel and the Post Office, both built in 1863. Today Yackandandah is a vibrant town of artist galleries, antique shops, cafes and country pubs, wide bluestone gutters and beautifully preserved buildings which echo the charm of bygone days, a time when legend claims notorious bushranger Daniel Morgan was seen fleeing through its hills on a stolen racehorse.

You can acquaint yourself with Yackandandah's famous main street by picking up a copy of the 'A Walk in High Street' flyer from the Visitor Information Centre. Learning about the buildings and their history while pausing for lunch, visiting the museum or admiring work by local artists are also popular. The gold mining heritage of the area is revealed with a visit to the Yackandandah Gorge or a tour of the Karrs Reef Gold Mine. You can even buy a Miners Right and seek your riches panning in Clear Creek. For those who enjoy their folk music and markets a visit in late March for the annual Yackandandah Folk Festival is a must.

Left: The site of Samuel Cunningham's store in the 1850s, the Yackandandah Motor Garage has also been home to a carriage showroom and over time, the gallery for a number of local artists and antique shops.

Below: Yackandandah is set amidst a landscape of rolling hills, state forest and open farmland. Take your time and explore the surrounding area, discover where dirt roads lead and with a little luck, you may just see an echidna.

BEECHWORTH

As you walk through Beechworth's historic precinct on a sunny day, the champagne granite of the town's gold rush era buildings sparkle in the sun. The home to over 30 National Trust listed buildings, beautiful parks and streets that erupt in brilliant gold, orange and red hues in the depths of autumn, Beechworth is one of the prettiest and best preserved gold rush era towns in Australia. Initially known as Mayday Hills, David Reid grazed sheep in the area until gold was discovered in 1852 by one of his shepherds. Word spread quickly with thousands of miners soon descending from across the world. The settlement grew quickly from rough timber huts and canvas tents to a town that by 1860 had a gaol, hospital and lunatic asylum. Excess was not unusual, with Daniel Cameron's famous 1855 ride through town on a horse shod with golden shoes still re-enacted in the Grand Parade every Easter weekend.

A great way to start a visit to Beechworth is to purchase a Heritage Pass, which will give you access to the historic precinct and walking tours. Visitors can stand in the dock of the historic Courthouse, as Ned Kelly did during his committal trial in 1880, or discover the wonders of the Burke Museum, where the camel bag and pistol owned by Robert O'Hara Burke can be seen. Walking tours led by passionate locals visit special places around town, such as the apple box But But tree, while spinning yarns of yesteryear. There are also options to drive through the scenic gorge, visit Woolshed Falls or expend a little energy at the local mountain bike park.

Above: For a unique perspective of Beechworth explore the historic gorge where you will find walking tracks leading to cool rock pools, cascading creeks and stunning views.

Top left: Built in 1870 to replace an earlier timber structure, the Beechworth post office reflects a grandeur of bygone days. Only recently did the building close, with Australia Post moving to new premises.

Bottom left: Opening in 1860, Beechworth Gaol hosted a list of infamous figures including Ned Kelly, his mother Ellen and Harry Power the 'gentleman bushranger'. Now a museum, tours give an interesting insight into prison life.

Previous page: Built in 1875 from timber and then in 1877 from granite, historic Black Springs Bakery is just one of many roadside surprises waiting to be discovered as you explore the Victorian High Country.

BRIGHT

The beauty of the Ovens Valley has enchanted visitors since explorers Hume and Hovell passed through the area in 1824, with Hovell noting that it is "...as pretty a spot and as valuable as any I have seen since leaving home". First settled by pastoralists in the 1830s who introduced cattle and sheep, the region's population grew quickly with the discovery of gold in 1853. By 1859, the town of Morses Creek had been surveyed and in 1861 renamed Bright, after John Bright the British politician. Deserving of its picturesque name, Bright rests at the foothills of the Victorian Alps, surrounded by snow-capped mountains in winter while in autumn, its famous deciduous trees, which include liquidambars, poplars and maples, erupt in spectacular red and golden hues, bringing the town's streets and parks to life.

As has been the case for well over 100 years, Bright's location close to Mount Buffalo, Mount Hotham and Falls Creek has seen it become a gateway for people who love the outdoors. On a stroll through the town centre you will discover, amongst other sights, the town clock, lolly and ice cream shops. Bright's parks are a delight, particularly in autumn when fallen leaves crunch under foot while the Ovens River burbles in the background. Events and markets throughout the year are a celebration of Bright and the region's local produce with thousands flocking to the Autumn and Spring festivals. Get up close to history with a stroll through Bright's spectacular Canyon Walk, where interpretive signs give an insight into the gold mining days.

Above: Accessible by car from Bakers Gully Road, or a scenic hour-long return walk on a steep winding track from McFadyens Lane, Huggins Lookout offers spectacular views of Bright and across the Ovens Valley on a clear day.

Far right: Generations of children have enjoyed playing in the parks along the Ovens River. For many, the time spent swimming, fishing and building small dams in the river will be memories they carry for a lifetime.

Right: Planted with a variety of deciduous trees and just a short walk from town along the Ovens River, Bright's memorial Arboretum is full of stunning colours during the autumn months.

MOUNT BUFFALO

The story of Mount Buffalo began millennia ago, as magma deep below the earth's surface slowly cooled, forming granite. Over time the surrounding sedimentary rock eroded to expose the plateau with its peak, The Horn, rising to 1723 metres. Sweeping alpine meadows, graced by wildflowers in spring and snow in winter are set against towering granite tors, their dramatic forms at times lost eerily amongst the clouds. Gnarled snow gums lost to past fires slowly regenerate, while burbling streams meander across the mountain, with Crystal Brook plunging spectacularly as it meets the gorge escarpment. There is a sense of scale and majesty to Mount Buffalo which saw government geologist Edward Dunn describe it as a 'Garden of the God's' in 1907.

With so much to experience on Mount Buffalo, many choose to camp at Lake Catani amongst the snow gums, taking their time to explore the mountain. The historic chalet at Bent's lookout has sweeping views towards the Great Dividing Range, a particularly stunning location to view sunrise as the gorge escarpment often glows a deep red. From the chalet, you can get back to nature with the Gorge Heritage Walk (2.5km) or take a gentle stroll out to Lake Catani (4km). Great picnic locations can be found by the lake at the old Grossman Mill site or at the Horn (unsealed, winding road). If you love waterfalls, descend into the depths of the mountain and discover the charm of Ladies Bath and Eurobin Falls (1.5km).

Above: The Cathedral and Hump are two icons of the Mount Buffalo Plateau, with the Cathedral a popular destination for rock climbing. For a unique perspective of these remarkable formations, take the steep, narrow track from the Cathedral picnic area (2km).

Left: Built in 1910 and listed on the Victorian Heritage Register, the Mount Buffalo Chalet is a favourite with visitors to the mountain. Although its doors closed in 2007, the gardens are well maintained and spectacular during spring.

MOUNT HOTHAM

Four and a half hours drive from Melbourne, at 1862 metres above sea level Mount Hotham is one of the highest points within Australia's Great Dividing Range. This is an ancient land in which the Gunaikurnai, Duduroa and Jaitmathang people once gathered over summer, where wildflowers dance in the summer breeze, snow gums strain under the weight of winter blizzards and the endangered mountain pygmy-possums pass under the Great Alpine Road through the 'Tunnel of Love'. With the first accommodation on the mountain catering to diggers travelling along narrow packhorse tracks between the Omeo and Buckland Valley gold fields in the mid-1800s, Mount Hotham is now home to Victoria's highest alpine village, offering 320 hectares of ski terrain, 35 kilometres of cross country trails, 13 ski lifts and its own airport.

Those rising early can breathe in the fresh mountain air and watch a new day break as the first rays of sunlight dance across the Razorback and Mount Feathertop in the distance. With a network of walking trails branching out across the High Country, visitors can walk as little or as much as they like. You can meander amongst the snow gums of the village, book in for a guided day walk or, if you're prepared and experienced, trek out cross the Razorback to Mount Feathertop for an epic overnighter. As the chill of winter bites and snow settles on the ground, Hotham's ski lifts begin to turn. Whether tobogganing at wire plain, snow shoeing the back country, learning to ski on the Big D or testing nerves on a black run, there's always adventure waiting at Hotham.

■ Following page: Rising to 1922 metres above sea level, Mount Feathertop's lonely, windswept and at times, inhospitable peak is Victoria's second highest. With snow lingering in deep gullies on its summit well into spring, many romantically believe the remnant snow to resemble a feather.

Left: The first accommodation opened at Hotham Heights in 1925 when Country Roads Board employee and legendary gold miner Bill Spargo converted his depot into a chalet.

Top right: Long after the summer bushfires are forgotten, scars linger on the delicate alpine landscape.

Right: Once a narrow coach road, the Great Alpine Road has become one of Victoria's great drives with breathtaking views as it crosses Mount Hotham.

DINNER PLAIN

As you descend from Mount Hotham towards Omeo, the dramatic mountain landscapes with sweeping views give way to rolling plains and snow gum woodlands. It is here, at 1570 metres above sea level and a short 13 kilometres from Hotham, that you will find the alpine village of Dinner Plain. Inspired by the iconic cattlemen's huts of a century ago, Dinner Plain feels perfectly placed on the edge of the Alpine National Park, its architecture and construction of corrugated iron, stone and timber at one within the landscape. Opened in 1986, the village takes its name from days long gone, when the coach service operating between Omeo and Bright would break its journey on the plain for dinner.

Mild summers, spring wildflowers and winter snow add a touch of magic to the high plains, making the village a perfect base for year-round adventure. Visitors often head to the majestic Carmichael Falls or explore the network of trails stretching back to Mount Hotham, discovering snow gum woodlands and High Country huts along the way. You can travel by foot, horseback or mountain bike in the warmer months or experience the wonder of cross country skiing and husky sled dog tours during winter. For families, Dinner Plain has a wonderfully relaxed atmosphere with a beginner's ski run and toboggan slope offering the perfect introduction to winter sports.

Above: Dinner Plain is a vibrant year-round village covering 231 hectares of sub alpine land with a sleeping capacity of 4,000 beds and a permanent population of 200 residents.

Left: Dinner Plain has a number of dining options including restaurants and a classic country pub.

Following page: From a rough log gaol built in 1858 to the grand 'new' courthouse of 1893, Omeo's Justice Precinct reflects the town's development as an important administrative centre during the Victorian gold rush days.

FALLS CREEK

Resting on the edge of the Bogong High Plains, Falls Creek Village gazes out across the Kiewa Valley from amongst woodlands of twisted snow gums at 1600 metres above sea level. Only 45 minutes from Mount Beauty and resembling a scene from a fairytale on a cold winters afternoon, Falls Creek owes its humble beginnings to the construction of the Kiewa Hydro System. Workers on the hydro scheme, in addition to building Rocky and Pretty Valley Dams, built the first lodge in the area in 1948. A ski lift then followed in 1951 and today Falls Creek boasts a capacity of over 5000 beds, 14 ski lifts and 65 kilometres of cross country trails stretching out into the high plains.

Home to the famous Kangaroo Hoppet cross-country event, it is the magic of winter which draws many to Falls Creek. Featuring the Windy Corner toboggan slope, extensive range of beginner to advanced runs and terrain parks, lifelong memories are created on the snow amidst spectacular scenery. Visitors take in the regular Thursday evening fireworks from the Village Bowl and ski Wombat's Ramble under lights on Saturday after dark. As the snow melts and alpine grasses emerge from hibernation, the warmer months are equally delightful allowing other activities such as walking the Packhorse Heritage Trail, once used by High Country cattlemen, and fly fishing for trout in Rocky Valley Lake. For the adventurous, 40 kilometres of trails within the Falls Creek Mountain Bike Park await to be explored.

Left: Keen boarders head out for a few more runs before night falls, as fog shrouds the distant valley and a bitterly cold wind cuts across the higher elevations of Falls Creek.

Below: The picturesque Rocky Valley Lake stands at 1600 metres above sea level, making it the highest significant body of water in Australia. Home to the Mile High Dragon Boat Championships, the lake is perfect for fishing, kayaking and a lazy summer's afternoon picnic.

BOGONG HIGH PLAINS

The Bogong High Plains is a vast rolling wilderness plateau set against the backdrop of Mount Bogong and Mount Feathertop. At 1893 metres above sea level at their highest point (Mount Nelse), the high plains are an exposed and windswept landscape subject to extremes of summer bushfires and winter storms. Here grasslands and heathlands grow in shallow soil while groves of gnarled snow gums bare the scars of a harsh alpine life. People have long been visiting the high plains, with indigenous groups ascending during the summer months to feast on Bogong moths and participate in ceremonies. By the mid-1850s the legend of the High Country cattlemen began as local graziers drove their cattle up into the high plains, taking advantage of the plentiful feed as droughts took hold on the lowlands. In more recent times the development of the Kiewa Hydro Electric scheme has opened up and reshaped the high plains with the creation of the picturesque Rocky Valley and Pretty Valley lakes.

Easily accessible from Falls Creek during summer, you can comfortably explore the high plains by car, with Wallace Hut and Cope Hut just a short walk from the road, approximately 12 kilometres from Falls Creek. Walkers can explore the trails and meander amongst the snow gums on Heathy Spur (10km) or take in spectacular views across the high plains from atop Mount Nelse (10km). One of Australia's largest snow-covered areas, the high plains road and walking trails form part of Falls Creek's 85 kilometres of cross-country terrain during ski season.

Above: Walking is a wonderful way to explore the Bogong High Plains and reconnect with nature. Discover the huts of the High Plains, watch fish swim in crystal clear alpine streams and if you are lucky, you may see a mob of wild brumbies.

Left: As you cross the Rocky Valley Dam wall, it may feel like you have left the world behind and entered a landscape which radiates a wonderful sense of isolation. Take your time as you drive across the High Plains, as even the views from the road across heathland, stands of snow gum woodlands and distant valleys are spectacular.

Following page: Rising to 1986 metres above sea level, Mount Bogong is not only Victoria's highest mountain, but also the wildest and least forgiving. Named after the local indigenous word for 'Big Fella', Bogong's striking plateau and deep gullies can be seen from across the High Country, with great views from Mount Beauty and the Kiewa Valley Highway.

HIGH COUNTRY HUTS

As you explore the Victorian High Country you will quickly fall in love with the rustic and at times quirky huts which blend into the landscape amidst groves of twisted snow gums on windswept plains, nestled below the tree line on mountain spurs or sitting deep within valleys on picturesque river flats. In a wild and unforgiving landscape, where unexpected storms bring heavy rain, icy winds and blizzards, these shelters have frequently been life savers for those who, for over a century have ventured into this beautiful wilderness.

Icons of the High Country, huts come in all shapes and sizes, each with their own story and personality. Some like Wallace Hut, built by the Wallace family in 1889, provided shelter as they grazed their cattle on sweet alpine grasses during the summer months. Others are replicas of huts lost to summer bushfires or built as a backdrop for classic movies such as the iconic Craig's Hut on Mount Stirling. In some cases however, huts have been built in memorial to those who paid the ultimate price in a wild landscape, ensuring future adventures have shelter in time of need.

With huts such as Cope, Wallace, CRB and JB Plain situated close to the road, there is ample opportunity to explore and soak up a little history on an easy stroll through the High Country. If you just happen to be in the High Country on a cold, wet afternoon you might just appreciate a little respite from the weather in one of these gorgeous little buildings.

Above: 12km from Falls Creek and a 750 metre walk from the carpark, Wallace Hut is the oldest surviving hut of the Victorian High Country. Known affectionately as the 'Seldom Seen Inn', it rests almost hidden from view amongst the snow gums of the Bogong High Plains.

Right: Built in 1929 by the Ski Club of Victoria, Cope Hut was a forerunner to the modern village of Falls Creek. Luxurious compared to the old cattlemen's huts, a beautiful timber structure lies beneath its hard, corrugated exterior.

Following page: Built by the State Electricity Commission to house those working on the Kiewa Hydro Electric Scheme, Mount Beauty is a beautiful foothill town set on a picturesque pondage in the shadow of Mount Bogong. It is the perfect place to take to the air for a scenic helicopter flight.

MANSFIELD

The Mansfield Shire holds a special place in the hearts of Australians with the iconic Man from Snowy River movie filmed in the region. Based on Banjo Patterson's poem, it celebrates the legendary High Country cattlemen while showcasing the area's stunning beauty. First recognised as a rich grazing area by Andrew Ewan in 1839, as he passed through while tracking stray horses, Mansfield's origins lie in a humble blacksmith's shop which opened near Ford Creek on the boundary of four large pastoral runs in 1850. A year later, land was set aside and a new town surveyed, with lots going on sale soon after. Today, Mansfield is a vibrant tourist destination and gateway to the alpine resorts of Mount Stirling and Mount Buller. Where bullock teams once negotiated u-turns, picturesque parklands now run through the centre of town, lined by tempting bakeries, cafés and stores selling local produce and art waiting to be discovered.

Mansfield's heritage can be explored at the old Station Precinct, home to the historical society, indigenous scar tree and interpretive poles which offer a glimpse into the area's early days. With the Delatite River and Lake Eildon nearby, there are ample opportunities to get back to nature while casting a line. For the romantic at heart, hot air balloon rides enable passengers to watch the first sweet rays of sunrise dance across the landscape. If you love local produce you will be delighted by what the region has to offer at the local Farmers Market on the 4th Saturday of each month. It also goes without saying, adventure and exploration await on Mount Stirling and Mount Buller.

Above: When full, Lake Eildon's holds up to six times the volume of water found in Sydney Harbour, its scenic 500km shoreline meandering between Jamieson, Howqua, Bonnie Doon and Mansfield. Visitors to the lake can enjoy bushwalking, boating, canoeing and fishing.

Left: Mansfield Zoo is one of the region's hidden gems with meerkats, blackbuck antelope, wombats, dingoes and of course lions waiting to captivate the imagination.

Above left: Sergeant Michael Kennedy accompanied by constables Thomas Lonigan, Michael Scanlan and Thomas McIntyre rode out of Mansfield in October 1878 in search of Ned Kelly and his brother Dan; only McIntyre would return alive. A marble statue in the centre of Mansfield, paid for by public donations, honours their memory.

MOUNT BULLER

Leaving Mansfield behind, you will soon see Mount Buller's distinctive form rise above the rolling foothills and open farmland of the Howqua Valley. Known to the local Taungurung people as 'Marnong', explorer Thomas Mitchell named the mountain after Charles Buller of the Colonial office in 1835. For thousands of years, the Taungurung and other indigenous people gathered here during summer, with ancient axe heads discovered high upon the mountain a reminder of their annual visits. By the early 1900s, Buller's potential as a tourism destination had been recognised by local grazier Frank Klingsporn, who improved access by upgrading an old cattlemen's trail. By 1929 the first chalet had been built on the mountain, but it would be another 20 years before the first ski tow would turn, leaving early adventurers walking to the top of each run before skiing down. Today, the resort has grown substantially, offering 2 toboggan runs, 3 terrain parks, 22 lifts, 300 hectares of skiable terrain and an overnight capacity of 7,000 beds. Car access is restricted during ski season: a free shuttle bus ferries visitors from the car park into the heart of the village. A perfect winter's day may start with a sled dog tour, followed by hitting the slopes, with 'Bourke Street' awaiting beginners and black runs on the southern side of the mountain ready to challenge experienced skiers. Summer brings a change of pace, with mountain biking terrain for all levels of ability and walking trails with stunning views awaiting bushwalkers and trail runners. For an insight into the history of the alpine region, pay a visit to Buller's National Alpine Museum of Australia.

Top: From Queens Birthday weekend, with visitors arriving from around the world, Mount Buller's village is full of life. With a cinema and over 30 restaurants and bars, there is plenty to keep you entertained.

Above: Keep an eye out for a little magic in the High Country. When you see this sign, something special is coming up a little down the road.

Left: Standing at 1805 metres above sea level the 360° views from the top of Mt Buller are stunning.

MOUNT STIRLING

IN amed after surveyor James Stirling and a little over 3½ hours from Melbourne, Mount Stirling lies just to the north of Mount Buller, separated by the Delatite River which rises to the east and flows to the west. Unique amongst Victoria's resort mountains, Mount Stirling is free from large scale development, with just a handful of refuge huts and Telephone Box Junction (TBJ), home to a toboggan run, café, ski hire and the Ski Patrol HQ which operates during winter. Offering visitors an alpine wilderness experience, Mount Stirling's rolling alpine meadows beg to be explored, its unspoilt summit rising to 1749 metres above sea level with 360° views across the High Country including Mount Buller, Mount Cobbler and the Crosscut Saw.

A year-round destination, Mount Stirling also has a wide range of trails which spread out across the 3000-hectare alpine area, suitable for bushwalking, mountain biking and horse riding. The unsealed and at times rough, Circuit Road starts at TBJ allowing exploration of the mountain by car during warmer months, with the Clear Hills 4WD track providing access to ever-popular Craig's Hut. Travelling by foot during winter is the only option and with snow settling on 68 kilometres of cross-country trails, a wonderful sense of isolation grips the mountain. Snow shoeing amongst the mountain ash, through snow gum woodlands and finally on towards the summit for a night of camping at Bluff Spur Hut is a physically demanding, yet delightful experience (12km return).

Above: Initially constructed as a set for The Man from Snowy River movie, Craig's Hut has earned its place in Australia's heart. Channeling the spirit of the Victorian High Country cattlemen and women, Craig's Hut is one of the mountain's most popular locations.

Right: Believed to be between 300 and 500 years old, the Mount Stirling 'Summit Tree' is a national treasure. A lonely figure above the tree line, the 'Summit Tree' has reached a remarkable size for a snow gum growing at an elevation of 1725 metres above sea level.

LAKE MOUNTAIN

You may be surprised to learn there are no lakes to be found at Lake Mountain, which takes its name from George Lake, a former surveyor-general of the area. Set within the Yarra Ranges National Park, Lake Mountain's summit rises to 1433 metres with lookouts towards the Great Dividing Range and over Marysville. Heavily impacted by the Black Saturday fires of 2009, the snow gums which cover the mountain's plateau make for a stark image as they slowly regenerate. Blue skies and over 90 species of wildflowers bring colour to the landscape from spring to early autumn, while snow and fog create a wonderland shrouded in mystery during winter. A pleasant 2-hour drive from Melbourne, passing through the Black Spur and picturesque town of Marysville, Lake mountain is popular for day trips throughout the year, recording the highest winter visitor numbers of any ski resort in Australia.

A premiere cross-country resort, with 37 kilometres of trails stretching out across the plateau, winter exploration on snow shoes or skis is a delight. A family-oriented mountain, kids can learn to snowboard, tackle the toboggan runs or launch through the air on a 240 metre flying fox while mum and dad enjoy a coffee from the nearby kiosk. Spring heralds the beginning of the walking season with the Summit (900m) and Summit Loop (4km) being popular shorter walks, while the Day Loop Walk (14km) offers a more intimate exploration of the mountain. For those completing the 7 Peaks ride, Lake Mountain offers one of the more challenging but rewarding climbs in the alpine region.

■ Previous page: Nestled in a pocket of rainforest, the Taggerty Cascades can be accessed by a short, steep 20 minute walk from the car park on Lady Talbot Drive, near Marysville. If you are lucky, you may even see lyrebirds as you explore the area.

Above: The Village Run is the most popular of Lake Mountain's two toboggan slopes. Equipped with a magic carpet, it is also the closest to the village with day shelter, kiosk and rental facilities nearby.

Left: With little infrastructure on the mountain, the only way to explore the area is by foot. Lace up the walking boots, hit the trails and discover the magnificent views which Lake Mountain has to offer.

MOUNT BAW BAW

With an annual rainfall average of 1500mm, the Baw Baw plateau is one of the wettest locations within the state of Victoria. Often enveloped by mist, it seems fitting that the ancient Woiwurrung people knew Baw Baw as bo-ye, meaning 'ghost'. One of seven peaks on the plateau, Mount Baw Baw is a subalpine landscape rising to an elevation of 1567 metres, with cool temperate rain forest to its south while snow gum woodlands and alpine meadows grace its higher elevations. Colour abounds in summer as wildflowers bloom while snow gums shed their bark in autumn, their beautiful reds and greens contrasting against the muted tones of winter. A region of ecological significance, the critically endangered Baw Baw frog lives amongst its wet forests and sub-alpine heathlands in a struggle against extinction.

Just 120 kilometres from Melbourne, Melbournites and other visitors can experience the thrill of a husky sled ride, take on the mountain's 25 ski runs or get out amongst the snow gums on 10 kilometres of groomed cross country trails. Be sure to stop by the Dingo Resource Centre any time of year where you can meet the adorable Rowdy and Warragul while also learning about the Baw Baw Frog. Walking trails beckon during the warmer months with spectacular views atop the Summit walk (2.5km, medium difficulty), while the fit and well prepared can spend 3 nights camping out as they explore the first 40 km of the Australian Alps Walking Track, hiking from the historic township of Walhalla to Mount Baw Baw.

Above: Mount Baw Baw's resident dingos, Rowdy and Warragul taking time out for a little snow play.

Below: The Baw Baw Plateau is the remnant of an ancient magma chamber which formed beneath the earth's surface and has been revealed over the ages as the land uplifted and surrounding rock eroded.

Far left: Mountain bikers will love the cross country and downhill descents from the alpine resort, while road cyclists will discover the ascent from the lowlands to be one of the most challenging climbs in the High Country.

ACKNOWLEDGEMENTS

The author would like to thank all the gifted photographers whose work is featured here. He would particularly like to thank Cristina Baccino, Craig Lewis, Ben Appleford and Craig Sheather. Chris would also like to thank Andrew Swaffer for his patience, guidance and commissioning the series; Christine Schiedel who has beautifully laid out this book; Jenny Cowan for the map. Thanks to the Burke Museum, Mansfield Zoo and Mount Baw Baw Alpine Resort for their images and assistance. Love always to Mum, Dad and brother Anthony.

ABOUT THE AUTHOR

Chris Munn is an author and freelance photographer. He is the co-author, with Craig Lewis, of Alpine Australia - A Celebration of the Australian Alps and author of Australian Geographic: Great Ocean Road. Based in Yackandandah at the foothills of the Victorian High Country, Chris spends much of his time exploring and photographing his 'back yard', Falls Creek, Mount Hotham and Mount Buffalo. When away from the camera, Chris is an avid runner who competes in 10-kilometre and half marathon events. www.chrismunngallery.com.

ABOUT THE PUBLISHERS

The Australian Geographic journal is a geographical magazine founded in 1986. It mainly covers stories about Australia - its geography, culture, wildlife and people - and six editions are published every year. Australian Geographic also publish a number of books every year on similar subjects for both children and adults. A portion of the profits goes to the Australian Geographic Society which supports scientific research as well as environmental conservation, community projects and Australian adventurers. www.australiangeographic.com.au.

Woodslane Press are a book publishing company based in Sydney, Australia. They are the publishers of Australia's best-selling walking guides and under their co-owned Boiling Billy imprint also publish camping, bush exploration and 4WD guides. For more than a decade committed to publishing books that empower Australians to better explore and understand their own country, Woodslane Press is proud to be working with Australian Geographic to produce this new series of souvenir books. www.woodslane.com.au.

Also available:

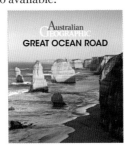 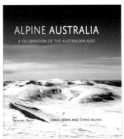 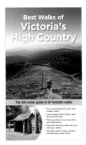

All images are protected by copyright and have been reproduced with permission.

PICTURE CREDITS

pi: Chris Munn (Bushwalker, Bogong High Plains)

pii: Shutterstock/Michael R Evans (Monarch Butterfly)

p1: Shutterstock/Ian Crocker (Farmland, Yackandandah)

p2-3: Chris Munn (Old Shed, Mudgegonga); Shutterstock/Phillip Allaway (Kangaroos)

p5: Cristina Baccino (Fainter Falls); Shutterstock/gordotkt (Great Alpine Road)

p6-7: Chris Munn (Basalt Formation); Shutterstock/Ian Crocker (Woolshed Falls)

p8-9: Chris Munn (Buckland Valley)

p10-11: Burke Memorial Museum (Barrow Derby); istock/photosbyash (Chinese Burning Towers)

p12-13: Shutterstock/FiledIMAGE (Howqua Valley); Shutterstock/deb22 (Snowboards)

p14-15: Craig Sheather (Mansfield Scarred Tree)

p16-17: Cristina Baccino (Gang-gang Cockatoos); Australian Geographic/ Ego Guiotto (Bogong Moths)

p18-19: Anthony Munn (Kookaburra); Ben Appleford (Brown Snake); Chris Munn(Koala); Shutterstock/ Deb Talan (Brumby)

p20-21: Chris Munn (Liquidamber); iStock/ photosbyash (Alpine Everlasting); Chris Munn (Snow Gum)

p22-23: Shutterstock/Nils Versemann (Yackandandah Motor Garage); Chris Munn (Echidna)

p24-25: Chris Munn (Black Springs Bakery)

p26-27: iStock/FiledIMAGE (Beechworth Post Office); Chris Munn (Beechworth Gaol); Chris Munn (Cascades)

p28-29: iStock/tsvibrav (Huggins Lookout); Chris Munn (Memorial Arboretum); iStock/FiledIMAGE (Splash Park)

p30-31: Chris Munn (Cathedral/Hump); Australian Geographic/ Don Fuchs (Chalet)

p32-33: iStock/colleenbradley (Hotham Heights); Chris Munn (Sunset); iStock/ the_apostrophe (Great Alpine Road)

P34-35: Chris Munn (Mount Feathertop)

p36-37: Chris Munn (Dinner Plain Village); Chris Munn (Restaurant)

p38-39: Chris Munn (Omeo Courthouse)

p40-41: Chris Munn (Boarders); iStock/tsvibrav (Rocky Valley Lake)

p42-43: Chris Munn (Sunset); Chris Munn (Bushwalker)

p44-45: Chris Munn (Mount Bogong)

p46-47: Chris Munn (Wallace Hut); Chris Munn (Cope Hut Interior)

p48-49: iStock/tsvibrav (Mount Beauty)

p50-51: Chris Munn (Memorial); iStock/ tsvibrav (Lake Eildon); David Hibbert (Lion)

p52-53: istock/FiledIMAGE (Sunset); Shutterstock/ annarevoltosphotography (Village); Shutterstock/Alizada Studios (Gnome Sign)

p54-55: Chris Munn (Craig's Hut); Chris Munn (Summit Tree)

p56-57: Sean Farrow (Taggerty Cascades)

p58-59: Shutterstock/Adrian Monoang (Tobogganing); Craig Sheather (Lookout)

p60-61: Shutterstock/katacarix (Village); Mount Baw Baw Alpine Resort (Dingos); iStock/Kevin Wells (Granite)